Praise for
What an Island Knows

"There is so much to celebrate in Alexander Levering Kern's new collection! (Because I don't know where else to say this, so here I'll urge you to read "After Fourteen Years," as beautiful an elegy as any you'll see). The book itself is celebratory, especially of the miracle of family life, always rendered with a flawless eye for detail: back at their summer retreat in coastal Maine, say, he notes 'the clicking of Legos / on the hardwood floor / as our children create a new world.'

"But although Kern is ever grateful for his blessings, what crucially ballasts *What an Island Knows* is its awareness of those who cannot celebrate, of 'a gasping world, survivors of war, / caravans of children, the widow, the orphan / ... a lone refugee climbing parched gullies / knocking on our door at night.' To me, important poetry always illustrates human maturity. Look at this wonderful collection. In its case, at least, you may well agree."

SYDNEY LEA, former Poet Laureate of Vermont;
Pulitzer Prize finalist; and founding editor
of *New England Review*

❋

"This gorgeous new book from Alexander Levering Kern stuns with its illumination of both the natural beauty of an island off Maine and the days of a family's summer stays there. We watch as children grow and parents age, each moment savored and beheld with love and a 'certain species of mercy.' From past wars to present ones, from brand-new parenthood to the hard losses life brings, Kern never fails to 'gaze into the heart of things.' Grandparents and earlier days in the Blue Ridge Mountains, the Indigenous peoples who lived on this island, its current-day elders and dogs, church choirs and black-eyed Susans—the poet lets them all speak. Reading these poems feels like the joy of intimacy, of gazing into a human heart always tilting toward true north and the eternal Beloved."

Donna Baier Stein, award-winning author
and founder/publisher of *Tiferet Journal*

※

"*What an Island Knows* is a beautiful love poem to a place—its myths and rhythms, histories and timelessness. Alexander Levering Kern takes us on a pilgrimage to his beloved Chebeague Island in Maine, sharing poem postcards filled with reverence for the ocean, its creatures, and tides. In these poems we encounter luna moths, fireflies, and the music of the Beatles. Here we meet Kern's Quaker ancestors and honor the footsteps of the Wabanaki people. 'We are ritual people,' the poet tells us, all the while inhabiting memory and rituals of belonging and homecoming. This enchanting book fills us with the motion of the tides, the birth of children, and the insistent call of summer. The 'ocean of memory' is at once filled with song and the memory of those departed. The poet inhabits his love of the world yet is conscious of its dangers and damage. Kern leads us home to a gentle silence, until we come close to the Divine and 'rise into (our) own liberation.'"

Deborah Leipziger, poet and author of *Story & Bone*

※

"In *What an Island Knows*, Alexander Levering Kern offers a memoir through place and family: a young man falls in love, builds a life, has children, grows older, and returns each summer to the same setting—Chebeague Island, Maine. Here, the landscape grounds us in wonderful particulars—weather, vegetation, children's games, webs of generations. The poems of fatherhood are especially moving. With his keen eye, Kern notes the way these particulars connect present to past and future, peace to war, growth to decline. 'Oh giver of water, giver of life, / teach us to pray / in streams of mercy for the news before us: / a gasping world, survivors of war, / caravans of children, the widow, the orphan, / the sign of coyote, the one who can't breathe,' Kern writes. But if the poems are always aware of suffering, they return again and again to prayer, hope, and a celebration of the dance of language and time: 'Why not teach the shadows to dance? / Why not simply sit and watch / the island roses begin to bloom?'"

    NADIA COLBURN, PhD, poet, author of *I Say the Sky*, and founder of Align Your Story Writing School

※

"Self-reflection, identity, heritage, fatherhood, family, friends, faith, and music—Alexander Levering Kern's debut collection of poems, *What an Island Knows*, is a love story of language and experiences. In 'Soundings from Chebeague,' readers are asked, 'If an island could speak, what might it say / and if listening, what might we hear?' The answer—it seems to me—after beachcombing every beautifully measured stanza in this book, is wind, saltwater, and poetry. Here, in these pages, Kern taps into a universal truth: life is a sacred journey."

    GARY RAINFORD, poet, author of *Adrift*, and editor-in-chief of *The Island Reader*

※

VOICES FROM CHEBEAGUE ISLAND, MAINE...

"Maine's year-round island communities are an endangered species. In 1900 more than 300 island hamlets dotted the coast of Maine, but today only 15 remain. Through his poetry, Alexander Levering Kern describes the importance of family, ritual, and renewal, which helps to explain why an island like Chebeague flourishes while others fade away. The poems remind us of the importance of finding the present in the past and the past in the present, as we look to the future. After reading Alex's book, I realized that it is this sense of place that has rooted my family to Chebeague Island for more than 250 years."

Donna Miller Damon, former curator of the Chebeague Island Historical Society and Museum, freelance author, contributor to *Working Waterfront*, former educator, and eighth-generation Chebeague islander

※

"'If once you have slept on an island / you'll never be quite the same,' so wrote poet and novelist Rachel Field almost one hundred years ago. Well, I have slept on an island, Great Chebeague Island, in fact, the setting of Alexander Levering Kern's *What an Island Knows*. Indeed, in just a couple of months Mhairi, my wife, and I will haul our suitcases, bags, and assorted boxes and cartons on and off the shuttle bus, along the weary dock, and down the steep gangway to board the ferry, *Independence*, and launch our fifty-fifth summer on that enchanted island.

"Yesterday, however, immersed in Alex's magical book of spells, it was as if I had never left the place. In scene after scene, moment upon moment—the shore, the woods, the velvet night sky, yes, even the luna moths and mosquitos—I was transported into an alternate reality without the need for any technological device at all. I knew once again the peace, the beauty, the sheer blessing of this 'demi-paradise,' this 'precious stone set in the silver sea'—Chebeague. I thank Alex, and all the powers that be, for at least one afternoon—still held within Maine's long and lingering winter—redeemed, lost and then found again along the rocky strands, the wandering paths and roads, the scented woodland trails, the creaking, comforting old cottages of our cherished Island of Many Springs."

J. Barrie Shepherd, poet, author, and retired Presbyterian minister

"Just what is it about Chebeague Island that captivates the heart? Just what is it that brings the devoted back summer after summer? What brings a ready smile to the lips of the year-round Chebeaguers when asked, 'What do you think makes Chebeague a treasured isle?' Many have tried to offer answers. Now I recommend that the reader settle down with Alex's poems. This is a wonderfully eclectic mix, and they are bound to resonate. Why do we love that special place? Kern's poems offer glimpses that satisfy."

ANDREW PHILLIPS GRANNELL, author of *A Lifetime of Good Beginnings: Stories Exploring Promise* and former Dean of the Earlham School of Religion

What an *Island Knows*

poems by
Alexander Levering Kern

foreword by
Betsy Sholl, Former Poet Laureate of Maine

SHANTI ARTS PUBLISHING
BRUNSWICK, MAINE

What an Island Knows

Copyright © 2024 Alexander Levering Kern
All Rights Reserved

No part of this document may be reproduced or transmitted in any form or by any means without prior written permission of the publisher, except where permitted by law.

Published by Shanti Arts Publishing

Designed by Shanti Arts Designs

Cover image: Walter Elmer Schofield, *Summer Afternoon, Chebeague Island*, c. 1923. Oil on canvas. 36 x 40 inches (91.4 x 101.6 cm.) Private collection. Wikimedia Commons. Public Domain.

Shanti Arts LLC
193 Hillside Road
Brunswick, Maine 04011
shantiarts.com

Printed in the United States of America

ISBN: 978-1-962082-25-9 (softcover)

*For Rebecca, Elias, and Ruthanna,
Beth, Michael, and the Grunko and McCullough families,
and all the people of Chebeague Island, Maine,
past, present, still to come*

Contents

Acknowledgments 15
Foreword by Betsy Sholl 19

I

Passage Over 25
Quality of Light 26
What Binds Us to This World 27
Chebeague Is an Abenaki Word 28
The Bridges We Build 29
What You Find on the Beach 30
Mysterious Visit of the Moose 31
With Eyes to See 33
Found Art 34
Arrival on the Island 36
Big Dipper after Midnight 37
Story of the Sea 38
Fear of Drowning 39
At the Museum Exhibit of Island History 40
A Photograph of the Eben and Susan
    Littlefield Bates House 41
Island Sabbath 42
Rainstick 44
Of Islands and Loss 46
After Fourteen Years 47
Dreams of the Whisper 48
The Etymology of "Actually" 49

II

The Hum of the World 53
Summer of the Snapping Turtle 54
Target Practice at the Beach 56
Dance along the Growing Edge 57
Waking Hour on the Island 58
Liberation of the Beached Whale, Mulling Vocation 59

Of Raccoons, Moons, and Other Creatures of the Night	60
Missing the Child Who Cries for Justice	62
Fireworks over Portland	64
The Renewal of All Things	65
Spirits of the Island Cottage	66
The House That Elias Built	68
Small Wildlife Observed While Sitting with Ruthanna on an Island Lawn	69
Cave Painting	70
The Varied Meanings of Green	71
Tethered	72
To the Tipi in the Island Meadow	73
Tibetan Prayer Flag	74
The Empire of Sister Monkey	75
Our Son's Ninth Birthday, Observed with Chinese Poetry	76
Pondering July as the Light Crawls across the Grass	78
My Daughter Ruthanna's Names for Snails on a Hike to Little Chebeague Island	79
Lost on the Little Island	80

III

Awaiting the Doctor's News	85
Coming to Terms	86
Some Things I Know to Be True	87
Family Health Crisis, Day Three	88
Pearl of Great Price	89
Anatomy of Yes	90
Soundings from Chebeague	92
The Pie Sale Fundraiser	94
World in Flight	95
Grandparents, Salvaging	96
Providence Chooses the Great Blue Heron	97
Vacation Choreography, Extended Family	98
Mystery	99
Secret Dreams	100
Vertigo-Proof	101
Living History	102
Unknowing at the Shaker Village, and Other Secrets of Maine	103

Rope Swing	105
Life of the Insects	106
Luna Moths Visit the Island Cottage	107
Old Dog Days	108
Supper with You	109
Dignity of Work	110
What Lives in the Winter Wall	111
Their Quiet Bedrooms	112
Quaking Aspen	114

IV

Jazz Trio at the Island Church	119
The Soul Put Back Together	120
The Peacemakers	121
What the Mountains Say	122
Captain Watches the Stars	123
Whiteness Afloat on Summer Vacation	124
Continental Divide	126
The Ferry to Other Islands	127
Deliver Us to Long Island, Maine	128
Emergency Mission	129
Island Rescue	130
What the Body Does	131
Island Archaeology	132
Self inside Self	133
Nighttime before the Sea Levels Rise	134
The Climate of Maine	135
"Abide with Us, For It Is the Evening": American Haiku	136
Departure	137
Beneath the Waves	138
Drop Me in the Water	139
Morning Prayer, Chebeague Island, Maine	140
Listen to Your Life	141
The Shape of Gratitude	142
The Island's Reminder	143
Notes	145
About the Author	151

Acknowledgments

A book of poems is finally the work of many hands. I want to thank the following people, places, and institutions for their care, support, and endless patience—and for helping these poems find a home in the world:

- the island of Chebeague in the Casco Bay of Maine—the sacred place where these stories unfold;

- the ancestors, elders, and citizens of the Wabanaki Confederacy (the People of the Dawnland or People of the First Light) who have stewarded the lands and waterways of Maine from time immemorial. I stand in awe of their legacy of cultural survival, resistance, and creative expression;

- my beloved family, especially my wife, Rebecca Grunko, and my children, Elias and Ruthanna Kern; my in-laws, Beth and Michael Grunko, who make a home for us all; members of the extended Grunko/McCullough family who fill cottages and tents on Chebeague each summer; my mother, Dr. Montague Levering Kern, my father, Charles E. Kern II (1934-2020), my brothers, Christopher and Deane Kern, and the wider Kern, Levering, Lindsey, Barbour, and Merritt families;

- the residents of Chebeague, especially the Chebeague Island Church, Historical Society, Library, and Transportation Company, and our late beloved librarian, Deborah Bowman. May her light shine on and her memory be a blessing;

- Christine Brooks Cote of Shanti Arts Publishing—the wonderful publisher, editor, and designer of this book;

- the poets and writers Betsy Sholl, Sydney Lea, Deborah Leipziger, Nadia Colburn, Donna Damon Miller, Gary Rainford, J. Barrie Shepherd, and Andrew Phillips Grannell, for all their encouragement and generous words of endorsement;

- my extraordinary colleagues at Northeastern University's Center for Spirituality, Dialogue, and Service—especially Sagar Rajpal, Soo Laski, and Ryan Jenkins—and our students, especially those engaged with publishing: the amazing Megan Chong, Lawrence Lai, Caitlin Ark, Racquell Bethell, Michael Bronson, Andre Dangi, Alex Goutier, Euponise Loiseau, Clark Luckhardt, Julia Mariano, Kiara Masaoy, Conor McLeod, Gaby Murry, Brianna Nesbeth, Sharan Sekhon, Dylan Soth, Yuandi Tang, Jayla Tillison, and Lauren Yoon;

- my fellow editors, contributors, and readers of *Pensive: A Global Journal of Spirituality and the Arts* [www.pensivejournal.com];

- fellow poets, artists, writers, mentors, and dear friends Cecilia Akuffo, Harrison Blum, Michael Boover, Matilda Cantwell, Matt Carriker, Eileen Cleary, Lin Feng, Ori Fienberg, Jeffrey Fine, Donna Hakimian, James Hannon, Chris Hosea, David Huddleston, Gila Lyons, Brother Jonathan Maury SSJE, Patrick McGlamery, Steve Novick, Chloe Noll, Abraham Schechter, Latoya Staine Carriker, Patricia Wild, and the inspiring Parents Nursery School crew;

- the beautiful places of retreat, writing, and community that have nurtured this book: Andover Newton Theological School (now Andover Newton Seminary at Yale Divinity School); Friends Meeting at Cambridge, Massachusetts; the Episcopal monastery of the Society of St. John the Evangelist; the New England Poetry Club, Bagel Bards, and the wider poetry community of greater Boston; Guilford College in Greensboro, North Carolina; Pendle Hill Study, Retreat, and Conference Center in Wallingford, Pennsylvania; Cooperative Metropolitan Ministries and RUAH Interfaith Spirituality Institute; the Glen Workshop of *Image* magazine (thank you, Gregory Orr); the Southampton Writers Conference; the homes/retreats of Gustav Peebles, Ben Luzzatto, Kurt Strunk, Janeanna Chapman, John Bucheit, and their families; and the T. S. Eliot Foundation and T. S Eliot House (The Downs) in Gloucester, Massachusetts, which provided an invaluable writer's residency at just the right time (a special thanks to Dana Hawkes, Claire Reihill, and Mary Rhinelander);

- the annual Writers Workshop of the William Joiner Institute for the Study of War and Social Consequences at the University of Massachusetts Boston, especially my teachers Martha Collins, Martín Espada, Danielle Legros Georges, Fred Marchant, Brian Turner, and Bruce Weigl;

- teachers and mentors who have shaped my practice of spirituality, the arts, and activism: Max Carter, Carole Treadway, Deborah Shaw, R. Melvin Keiser, Joe Groves, David Landis Barnhill, Adrienne Israel, Judith Weller Harvey, Sister Helen David Brancato IHM, Mark S. Burrows, Lonnie Edmonson, Sally Selby, Mark Heim, and Robert Pazmiño;

- Donna Baier Stein, beloved teacher, editor, and publisher of *Tiferet* magazine, and our dear colleagues in her weekly spiritual poetry group;

- all those who advocate for poetry in New England and beyond, including the Maine Writers & Publishers Alliance, Mass Poetry, and *The Island Reader;*

- the editors of the publications in which some of these poems first appeared, sometimes in slightly different forms: *About Place Journal, Friends Journal, Ibbetson Street, JAMA: The Journal of the American Medical Association, Poetica, Spare Change News, Soul-Lit: A Journal of Spiritual Poetry, Sunday, The Aurorean, The Bagel Bards Anthology, The First Day, The Island Reader,* and *The Sloop's Log*;

- and you, dear reader—may you too find a home in these pages.

Foreword

I've come to think of Alexander Levering Kern's beautiful book of poems, *What an Island Knows*, as a kind of Book of Hours, or Book of Days, a pilgrim's log tracing a journey that is both communal and profoundly interior. With a light touch, Kern makes each poem delicate and moving, as he chronicles his many summers on Chebeague Island, Maine. Year-round residents, of course, can be ambivalent about summer people, but not those like Kern with his long history and deep respect for the land, who approaches his time there with humility and gratitude. The music of his poems and their fresh eyes are gifts for the whole community.

For a poet, language is a form of seeing, and these poems give us a clear and stunning lens to look at "riven clouds and grapefruit sun," or a snapping turtle "gray as Spanish moss and large as a hubcap," or mosquitoes "buzzing our ears like the electric guitars of the punk rock gods." I could go on and on with these delights, but here is one more—gazing at the night sky, he gives us "the silver syrup of galaxies." That, you can almost taste.

One strand running through these deeply humane poems is delight, or better yet a kind of cherishing. It starts with attention, which Simone Weil calls a form of prayer. We find that immersion in Kern's close attention to the land and its history, to the rounds of the tides and of day and night. There is also a profound attention to fatherhood in poems that deeply cherish a son happily constructing ballparks, a daughter utterly trusting a zip line built by her grandfather. Family is present in larger circles as well—uncles, aunts, grandparents, cousins, and beyond that the larger island community.

"No man is an island," John Donne tells us, and in a sense these gentle, probing poems suggest no island is an island either, if by island we mean an isolated place cut off from the world, an escape from self or history. For Kern an island is a place of renewal, where the endless distractions and obligations of workaday life grow still, and a deeper reflection begins. Besides allowing time to breathe and be with the natural world and family, the island allows this poet to reflect on the tensions we each carry within and so often ignore for the sake of efficiency. Kern is not afraid of those darker strands. There is a beautiful elegy for a friend, and a moving sequence of poems expressing all the fears around a health crisis. There is also family history, including the poet's mix of abolitionist and enslaver ancestors. There is the history of the island going back to its early Indigenous people and the current life of island community that itself becomes a character in these poems. One element that gives these poems their depth is Kern's ability to keep an undercurrent of the larger world's troubles washing up like the tides.

Among this book's many gifts perhaps the greatest is the poet's ability to express his—and dare I say our—interiority, as his attention to the natural world becomes spiritual and his awareness of humanity leads him to language of the divine. He can invoke the "God-language" of his grandmother, and what he calls "the Seed within," which come from his Quaker roots in ways that make the search for wholeness fresh and compelling. Walking along the shore, along island roads, into night fields with this poet becomes a journey toward the surrender of self-importance and relinquishment of fear. We come to embrace both self and other, shadow and light, and find that in the presence of God, of the sacred, even our wounds have become gifts.

These poems teach us to "navigate by mystery," like the old sea captains. Where else but on an island, just distant enough to change our perspective, an island where every cove and hill is known, with a broad sky and a sea full of history and erasure washing against the shore—where else to learn the fine art of gratitude and grace, to see how small we are and yet how utterly cherished?

BETSY SHOLL
Poet Laureate of Maine (2006–2011)

I

Passage Over

Like a nautical compass we long for true north
wherever that place may be. It's high tide
that draws us here: summer natives and islanders,
driftwood jettisoned from the mainland,
from every hidden corner of worry and need.

There's a collective exhaling we feel on the bus
that trundles us down to the ferry dock:
strangers, neighbors, familiar dogs
each sniffing for ocean air.

We are ritual people, loading and unloading
our common freight, hand over hand
like the solstice dance of a medieval village,
the weak always helping the strong.

Soon our luggage will rest in the ferry
and we'll nod and smile, unburdened for now.
The island waits, and when we reach the shore
we'll go our separate ways.

Quality of Light

In the hour before the red sun sings
the world awake, the seaweed, the tides,
      and the night conspire
to speak once more of familiar things
like the slow, swift march of the quality of light:
morning, midday, middle of life
dangling on the hook of a long afternoon,
riven clouds and a grapefruit sun,
blood at the roots and a hand reaching toward us,
seagrass like parchment, a shredded book,
the desiccated carcass of the harbor seal,
summer dying, summer rising again.

What Binds Us to This World

is not the tendon extending from heel to calf
the one I'd always feared would tear
nor the fickle magnet of gravity
nor the way we place our flags in dirt
on mountaintops in foreign lands.
Instead it's the gaze into the heart of things
the listening to the mystery
of the mourning dove and snowy owl
sheltering there behind the veil,
the soft of evening wrapping its arms
around the hamlet of our lives,
the play of light upon our eyes
weeping at the impermanence
a voice by the hearth telling the story
of mud and tide, aspen and pine,
and the search for common things.

Chebeague Is an Abenaki Word

meaning "island of many springs," some say,
this brook, for instance, beside the road
or the currents of words in the quiet of morning
streaming through a veil of ferns,
or the creeks that slake the thirst of gulls
whose stories recall the cascading jazz
of birdsong and frogs in the lavender hour
before sunrise, with island roses
and trillium swimming in private seas.

Oh giver of water, giver of life, teach us to pray
in streams of mercy for the news before us:
a gasping world, survivors of war,
caravans of children, the widow, the orphan,
the sign of coyote, the one who can't breathe,
a lone refugee climbing parched gullies
knocking on our door at night.

The Bridges We Build

I had never felt as cold as that day
in October I first visited the island in Maine
to bond with my girlfriend's family,
conscripted to help them build a bridge
across their frigid creek. All I really wanted then
was to huddle with Becca beside the fire
in their summer home beside the sea.
Instead, her father, a goateed union activist,
and her teenage brother, a long-distance runner,
asked me to join them out in the woods
with boards and tools to conquer the creek.

It wasn't exactly carrying a shovel to dig my own grave.
It reminded me more of my grandfather Sam,
how when my father asked for my mother's hand,
Sam paused for a moment, pursed his lips,
and suggested my father might consider instead
a few years with the Peace Corps in Indonesia.

Before too long, in spite of my clumsy hands and feet,
a bridge emerged above the lichen, mica, and fern.
In time, I became their family, a dweller in the land.
Generations of children now cross the bridge
between their house and the hardwood forest.
The wood we used turned shades of gray,
while the seagrass turns shades of green.

What You Find on the Beach

Rusted steel from World War II
on the submarine nets the navy used
to repel the German threat.

Sand dollars and cerulean seaglass,
wine bottles with secret messages,
deer bones and shards of china.

Stone tools used by the Wabanaki bands
to fish & clam, before returning to camp
and sell goods to tourists of the Gilded Age.

Unvanquished, they drank from freshwater springs
and when their clamming season was done
they left shells in middens that children discover

as they discover themselves, alive to the world
by the landbridge of sand that rises and falls
as the tides follow the moon.

Mysterious Visit of the Moose

In the meadow near the ruins of the Hamilton home
with its ancient granite and chimney hole,
crickets rubbed their brittle wings, watching the shadow
of a lone moose moving toward the island cottage
on the morning our son was born.

Imagine with me: a moose choosing to swim over
from the mainland, spider-like legs plowing past
colorful buoys as the ocean whispered,
A new child is coming into the world.

Did the island know then that down the coast
Becca's labor began before dawn? Did nature
remember how decades ago a zookeeper gave
my people the name "the Moose Family,"
gangly and comical as they were?

Could sunrise recall the Abenaki tale of the hero
Gluskabe encountering the primordial moose
who threatened to trample the humans and toss them
over his shoulders until the hero cried "No!"
and reached out to bend the moose's nose
and soften his belligerent spirit?

Did the spirit of my family home down in the Blue Ridge
visit the island in Maine that morning, rising up
from its ruins among the summer's cherry trees,
as our Quaker ancestors spoke their peace
in a time of unending war?

Did the moose know then that our son Elias
would grow into a wild and wacky boy
banging pots and pans on the kitchen floor
or that his first stab at humor would be a song:
"Really big moose, really big ears, tail on bum"?

Well, maybe it's the ravings of a first-time father,
but something inside me believes that the island
knew then that a new life would greet the blue heron,
the seal, the sea grass, the fox in her den.

Did the island lean in to hear the boy's cry?
Did the Blue Ridge rise up and sing?

With Eyes to See

The ancient sun was just barely peeking
its red nose through the evergreens
as I rose with my son—just a few weeks old—
to keep his wailing from waking his mother
and I held him—how I can feel it now—
delicate bundle of bones and breath—
and we glided quietly through a waking world
of the gray living room beside the sea—
the world-blurry forms of armchairs and couches
and cedar walls crawling, out from behind
the veil of dreams. In the rose-lit dawn
we sat on the porch overlooking the lilies
bidding the world *Good morning* and as you fussed
and mussed and howled just a bit, I held you
in your blanket and I swear on my grave,
after weeks of your eyes scouring the sky
and the ceiling fan and anywhere but mine,
you gazed into my eyes with fresh recognition,
bemusement, knowing there's an I and a you,
and something between us—and now, now,
these twenty years later, you look into eyes
of friends and strangers—no fear, only smile
and the hum of connection—your eyes,
        smiling and blue.

Found Art

There comes a time off the coast of Maine
when autumn smuggles its way into
the slumbering days of July.
The birds sense it before we do:
crows vie for rule of the roost
while hummingbirds wait in the wings.

Evening descends, pursing its lips at the grapefruit moon
as we board the ferry, hauling its catch of quiet souls,
leaving lobster boats and the good ship *Tuppence*
happy, adrift in its wake.

In the hold the islanders' faces glow
like jack-o'-lanterns and our toddler cries *No*
at the phantom ship's roar and the bad men
on horseback who haunt his dreams.

Night carries us over, a new day wakes
and before long a fog from the ocean creeps in,
pulling wool over the eyes of afternoon.
Blades of rain cut the front-porch horizon,
cross hatching with birches and aspens until
all distinctions bleed into one.

Woodsmoke mingles with cedar scent,
dancing along the cottage walls, as I watch
the waves of wildflowers crashing
over the meadow toward a toy ocean liner
sculpted from garbage heaps of the world:
bottle caps, whisks, and old plunger parts
careening through the green of our raspberry patch
in a riot of color to hold back the night.

Before too long the rains will subside and summer return
and with our eyes open wide, we'll see the world as it truly is:
our lives, yours and mine, a work of found art, a radiance,
      together in a little boat.

Arrival on the Island

Cottage doors swing open wide
as the fingertips of summer rain
play timpani on our shingled roofs.
Matches are struck, the fires lit,
and soon the braided beards of smoke
will wend their way toward heaven.

Indoors, our couches are little boats
drifting in forgetfulness, while down
by the wharf, among the buoys
and harbor seals, the ferry yawns,
inhaling the night and refugees,
souls afloat on other seas.

Big Dipper after Midnight

After the dishes are done and the fire is banked
and the denizens of night
have all retreated to their cocoons,
you can hear the dew forming in the trees,
tapping on the doors of leaves.

You steal outside and enter the cool green
nimbus of porchlight flooding the meadow,
reaching for the hands of the quaking aspens
past the tipi in its silent leaning.

It's then you look up and are overcome
by the vast Big Dipper filling the yard,
far greater than you've ever seen,
framed in the palm of spruce and oak.

In the time of the old astronomers,
these very stars looked down upon
your forebears' plantations in tidewater Virginia
yet also looked toward the light in the barn
where your Ohio Quaker ancestors waited
for other bondsmen crossing over Jordan.

Story of the Sea

>   —*Chebeague Island Historical Society*

My eyes scan the old documents
to learn about others' ancestors
from the island's trunk of history,
hoping to discover something of mine,
>   if only in a mirror.

One family, it seemed, would fish and trawl
for swordfish, sardines, herring, and clams
>   but never for lobster, they say.

Was it those pearly eyes, beady and dark,
the way they stare as if to say,
>   how could you do this to us?

Or was it their claws lashing the air,
or the fear of facing these ancient insects
>   when swimming too far in the deeps?

My eyes rove on to learn something more
of dory fishing—taking a little boat out to sea
with hoes, spears, harpoons, and hope—
and I'm wondering now

what weapons are required of us
to feed our people and keep us safe
from whatever would rise from the deep?

Fear of Drowning

How can I be so at home in this place,
surrounded by sea on an island in Maine?
—after all that is sunken in my family tree
like our wicked patriarch of Fitchetts Wharf
in the river marshes of tidewater Virginia—
a shipbuilder, enslaver, Confederate smuggler
through Union blockades, his son a trader in human lives
who was shipwrecked and drowned off the African coast.

What's more, there's my grandfather's hidden story:
a naval officer from Washington, D.C.
who sailed the Atlantic in the Suicide Fleet
during World War I, protecting supply lines
from German U-boats, carousing later
in Constantinople, then patrolling the Yangtze
to guard American ships, yet discovered himself
many years later, alone one evening, leaving a letter
before drowning himself in the C & O Canal.

As children we were told he'd developed a cramp
from swimming too soon after lunch. His son, my father,
showed no love for water, sinking like a stone, he said,
at his first swimming test, and I remember now
what it means to float on a summer lake, watching
my father stranded on tiptoes, calling out for help.
Some days even now I look to the ocean,
then quickly reach for the shore.

At the Museum Exhibit of Island History

The Ladies' Aid Society on Great Chebeague
is not so different from the way it was
in the 1940s, to hear Mrs. Audrey Collins
explain. They're still connected
with the Island Church, making old things new
as needs arise and the spirit leads.

Alongside their elders, so many are here
in the browning black-and-white photographs:
Hamiltons, Collinses, Komlosys, and Sweets
faces as strong as a winter in Maine, stronger
than the great gray granite slabs
their ancestors hoisted and hauled in sloops
down an unforgiving coast.

Here between these clapboard walls,
their quiet lives are stitched together
in crazy quilts, sewn in slender
wedding dresses, carved on chessboards,
hewn from eighteenth-century homes,
pulled from the soil, pulled up from the sea.

A Photograph of the Eben and Susan Littlefield Bates House

—circa 1878

The house still stands, the barn too,
near the place where South Road
veers toward Deer Point, beside a broken
clamshell path. In the photograph,
slightly askew, the Greek Revival stands.

In a long dark dress, a woman stands
beside an old mustachioed man,
an appropriate distance for modesty.
Nearby a younger woman watches
her children play beside the bones
of a whale washed up by the sea.

Its ribcage shines in the summer sun
and in that solemn instant, the young woman grins
defying all laws of photography
in the black-and-white nineteenth century,
but who could blame her, standing still,
her children frolicking among the bones?

Island Sabbath

It starts like this: a day so azure, so luminous
        in late summer stillness
it could be a Van Gogh canvas from Arles
but instead we're adrift on an island in Maine
drawn to the boatyard where a giant backhoe
digs its own shallow grave among the weeds.

Bright orange teeth puncture the earth
and vines scurry up to claim their seats,
strangling the gears and the steering wheel
as the skeleton frame and vacant arms
rust in peace and a white pine stencils
an epitaph for the end of summer.

In the bay below, rich boats and poor,
sailboats and skiffs, all bob and weave,
rising like molars from the maw of the sea.
Suddenly from the ocean of memory comes
a shaggy giant in Harvard Square, his teeth
decaying in blackened gums, his long trunk
swaying, his yellow beard wet with spit.
He bobs among bluebloods and fishermen
all in the soup of a slow dimming day,

    then pitches me a line, one I'd heard a thousand times,
    about needing money for a twenty dollar room
    after the local pastor said no. So now I wonder
    could not for once this island be island,
    vacation be sabbath, and the slow work of feeding the poor
    or healing the man with the withered hand
    be a nine-to-five job, a vocation for mainland life?

No, not yet, the answer comes. The poor we'll have with us,
even here, even now, and somewhere out there
in the ocean of night the fishermen will cast out
their nets once more, while here on the shore,
the backhoe is quaking and grinding its teeth,
rumbling into our lives.

Rainstick

With forked tongue, high tide licks the shore
jarring my body from midsummer sleep
while above me a great blue heron shrieks:
a pterodactyl careening from hell, dark wings
beating sense from the senseless,
       pulp from the rind of the sun.

My feet carve a way through a minefield of shells
and tombs of meat for ravenous gulls
while across the water a power plant wheezes
and the morning's news unfolds again:
       not far from here, a pilot died

a man who in 1945 flew over his target
but discovered cloudcover obscuring his view,
so abandoned that city and proceeded on
to Nagasaki, a diamond peering
       through an aperture in the clouds.

As his payload poured down,
       he cocked his head a bit to one side
             to watch the colors rise.

❋

Today in Maine, the Atlantic attacks the scarlet cliffs
and I remember the day we scattered the ashes
of grandmother Ruth, then sang the song she'd always sing
while riding the waves: a song of heaven and dancing
       and beating hearts, of happiness made whole.

A man of Ruth's time, the pilot trained in the deserts of Utah
where white sands trembled beneath the bomb.
On the day of his mission, the plane malfunctioned,
bleeding six hundred gallons of fuel into the sea.
The crew hurried repairs in time for the target
        and escaped with two minutes to spare.

The plane he'd piloted three days before
        to assess the damage to Hiroshima
                was called the *Great Artiste*.

❋

On the shore today, scabbards of mussel shells
cling to buoys, wind tramples the tall seagrass.
Missiles strike other deserts abroad,
while somewhere down in Mexico,
an old man sits, carving a rainstick
from a hollow cactus tipped on its head.
Pebbles pour down the interior,
a waterfall song in the night.

A thunderhead rumbles and I run for shelter
then wait in the shadows for the storm to subside
        and we're free to watch the rainbow rise
                over a place called Artist's Point.

Of Islands and Loss

So the island sun is setting now
across the skein of water,
an incandescent layer cake
of scarlet, fire, amber, rose.
High tide arrives on polished feet
framed in lavender, stitched in gold.
On the cottage porch long after dark
the talk's of this, the talk's of that.
By the edge of the meadow
the birches lick honey from the dark
with twilight tongues of loneliness.

A book of poems lies open before me,
the words spell forgiveness, recalling the loss
of our unborn one, still learning the heart drum,
still wearing a delicate mantle of nerves.

Here by the window all we can see
are the luna moths tapping their divining rods
while fireflies sketch melodies onto the darkness
and June bugs rap their knuckles against
the illuminated surface of our pane.

After Fourteen Years

—for Daniel Patrick O'Connor (1972–1991)

You're here in the wild
grin of brown boulders
along the jewel-crusted coast of Maine.
You're here in the panting
of the dog by my side,
in the way wind blows
through an empty blue bottle
like a flute from the Andes
or the high lonesome sound
of the Blue Ridge we once knew.
You're here in the quicksand
and the low groan of fog horns,
in the sharp scent of pine needles
returning to earth. You're the breeze
in a coffee mug, smiling improbably,
lying in wait on the path to the sea.
Walking this garden in the cool
of the evening, I find myself asking,
Where are you now? I know only this,
dear friend long departed:
you've poured out your life
into this luminous world.
There's nowhere now
you are not.

Dreams of the Whisper

Lying in the grass, deep-breathing the dusk
of a midsummer island, a riot of aspen
and teal-green sky, I dreamt of this:
neither image nor story but only a voice
in the God-language of my grandmother
whispering, *There is the Lord, looking at me.*

How strange it was to hear a dream
without a picture or a script, as if
the children's book of my life
had been clipped of half its meaning.

This had happened only once before:
in my year of shattering and coming home
after my friend Dan's death, as I slept
on my fourposter childhood bed,
its brown sheets patterned with hieroglyphs,
I dreamt a couplet, simply this:
>*As the horses make another round*
>*The plowman walks the furrowed ground.*

As I walk the middle way of my life
sometimes I hear the silence say,
Rise into your own liberation.
At other moments, a quiet comes:
Sink down, man-child, sink down to the Seed
to the green habitations of the heart,
to the one your Quaker ancestors knew:
the sower who sings in winter.

The Etymology of "Actually"

Actually, yes, the three-year-old replied
        when the librarian asked,
Do all your sentences begin with Actually?
Yes, as if the saying would make it so.
"Actually": a word so close to "factually"
and not far off
from the mighty acts of God.
Actually, my son believes
the Swedish Chef throws paintballs in the air
and the Red Sox play baseball in our backyard.
Actually, God wraps the fearsome
painted clowns and bad masked men
in a cloak made of night
and throws them gently into the sea.
Actually, the sunken walls all tumble down,
down beneath the waves.
Actually, the stars fall quietly in the northern sky.
Actually, it's Sunday morning in the island garden,
mosquitoes conspiring to claim our lives,
but in an instant now we'll all arise
to claim new faces. We'll all be changed:
Actually, impossibly, yes.

II

The Hum of the World

—for Ruthanna

Listen now to the far room calling
the cottage walls breathing
the breath of the baby
asleep on her quilts
the rumble of the earth's core
far beneath whales' song
falling into nightfall
rising with the first sun,
greeting of a new day,
greeting of a new world,
greeting of an island,
greeting of a blue dawn,
greeting of a child.

Summer of the Snapping Turtle

The year comets clashed in the northern sky
a turtle appeared at the end of our road.
Gray as Spanish moss and large as a hubcap,
she swiveled her head. Away, away, she seemed to say
but crowds gathered and wondered, Is it safe to move her?
No one could answer so we stood and waited
and I imagined her later, alone in the darkness.
Like my enemies, the foxes circled her nest.

In the kayak that evening I watched as my son
pulled handfuls of seaweed up from the deep.
"Lobsters," he'd say, and a riptide of fear
grabbed at my belly. We were out too deep
but our four-year-old pirate had taken command
crying "Further still! This way, and that!
Out to the *Osprey*, on to the *Dovekie*.
Keep paddling on to the setting sun!"

Earlier that summer in the seminary hallway
the inward voice whispered, *I will lead you if you let me.*
The ceiling lamp hummed, space-time dissolved,
and as if in a dream, I woke later in Maine
where the cedar walls taught me to breathe again,
whispering the names of those I could trust.

In the stillness before rising, one truth came clear:
someone I knew well desired to know me
but only in the power of my own resurrection
beyond snapping and fighting with terse word and silence,
out past the road where the word *MARS* hung low
in Christmas lights on a bleach-bone wall.

"God," our son Elias said, "is a criminal of peace"
and when I woke I learned they'd delivered the turtle
down past the clam shack, down to the fire pond,
down to where the cool rivers run
without murmur or regret.

Target Practice at the Beach

Sometimes there's no symbol, only comic relief.
Consider how, for a four-year-old boy,
an abandoned buoy becomes a target
of endless delight. Consider the swiftness
with which ammo flows from one intensity
into the next: first come cannonballs
of mud like scat, then rocks torn up
from the ocean floor, cracking on contact
like baseball bats. Then comes a log
that shatters swiftly into hundreds
of tiny impotent spears. We shout out loud
at each new hit, and truth be told
I feel no remorse, not even a dose
of good Quaker guilt. We're purged by the sun
and the thirsty waters, high tide lurching
like a drunkard at dinner, while off in the ocean,
the sea birds are laughing and high up above
the invisible stars whirl on as they will,
oblivious to our warring below.

Dance along the Growing Edge

Beware the wilderness of your heart,
a turkey picking across your lawn
indiscriminately gathering seed.

Beware the defenses you've locked inside,
the box turtle hunkered in his shell
waiting for his moment to pounce.

Beware your appetite to consume
all there is to be and do
with this one brief life we're given.

Beware the decisions teetering this way and that,
tightrope walker or acrobat,
fate unfurled at the end of a string.

But wait, hold on, there's more than this,
there's the Seed within, a surrender of self
that self might live abundantly

in the early morning time of dew—
wild roses climbing a driftwood trellis,
blossoming at the edge of your life.

Waking Hour on the Island

All day long my mind hung limp in the August haze,
an ox stalled in the road between then and not yet. Here sits
the magnificent chair; here too the lightning, my lantern.
Crabapples stare down the emerald void.
Raindrops purse their purple lips
all along the thin white rail.

Liberation of the Beached Whale, Mulling Vocation

A wild ox thunders through the screen of my mind
and I'm out on the beach with high tide rushing
through the barrier reefs
beneath my feet, while fallen leaves
      shadowbox across the sand.

Like baby's breath, the clouds exhale
blowing tall ships through Leviathan's sea
and I'm frozen here as the cartographer sleeps,
his old maps bleeding lavender ink
      across the parchment of my heart.

Stuck between the pincers of what's next & not yet,
I'm one day jumping on crocodile tails
the next day stranded flat on my back,
sand fleas crawling over my eyes,
      waves menacing my shore.

But today is different. I can see more clearly:
a lone boat drifting through surly waters,
its scarlet sail a tongue of fire, remembering the tale
of the early Quaker voyagers who in the midst of a storm
heard a voice implore them, *Cut a straight course now,*
      and mind nothing but me.

Of Raccoons, Moons, and Other Creatures of the Night

Oh to be an arrow on a string,
cut loose from any expectation
of who or what this man might be.
Now the arrowhead points to the sun
then to the far side of afternoon
where a harvest moon is swinging low
and the organ grinder inside my mind
is singing love songs as Sister Monkey
sings along: "Fly me to the moon," they sing,
before the warm breath of night exhales.

Oh, moon out prancing over the island
mirror image of the tangerine sun
gazing tenderly like lovers at dusk,
let your mind sink deeply into your heart
and abide there all day, as the old monk says.
Yours is the day, yours also the night,
your every motion is love.

Fearless now is the great raccoon,
bottom-wobbling down the forest path.
There's no shame, brother mammal,
in strutting your stuff: no audience needed,
no bugle blare. Just head up the steps,
up by your claws, up by whatever grace
made this world and keeps us still,
never leaves us to fate like yo-yos spinning
at the short end of a string.

Oh, wily old moon and soft summer sun,
don't leave me now to the talons of night.
Let me sing in time with your ravenous stars,
the song of the heron, the osprey, the deer,
all tethered to the world we love.

Missing the Child Who Cries for Justice

Baby Girl Ru, or "Thanna" as your brother calls you,
    Ruthanna is your true name.

How I adore the sound of your words, a poetic line:
    Ruthanna Julian Kern,
        all *uuu's* and *nnn's*, and your namesake

Julian of Norwich who knew that *All shall be well,*
    all manner of thing shall be well
        when I felt myself falling off the edge of the world.

I remember awakening to the sound of your cry
    in the shingled cottage beside the sea.

We called you Beloved Demon Baby
    as you trembled red, startling
        the mourning doves from their rest.

Now nearly one, you've claimed your breath:
    strong words coming, though not quite yet.

Your disgruntled scowl has receded now,
    replaced by the propulsive power of voice, a stiff neck raised
        against the injustice of an early bedtime,
            and the injury of a world at war.

This week you are there on the island in Maine
    and I am here, two states away,
        in a seminary summer camp, huddled with my others:
            teenage conspirators in the revolution of love

yet with candles lit, tonight I know
      that together we will make our way
           to the abundant oneness
                known first in the quiet of a baby's breath,

a pat on your back,
      your daddy's palm hovering, gently now,
           should you ever be afraid.

Fireworks over Portland

A waterfall of roses beyond the harbor
out past dawn, years gone by,
as our boy's grown tall
into a fearless new creation.

Scaling pines, shaggy and wild,
he's a watcher of things that lie below
where once he trembled in fear.

Watching him now, I remember as a child
a flickering sky, white lightning crashing
over our porch, all power out,
save for the candle in my father's hand.

Our son Elias now knows the terror
of watching a sky on fire.
From the flatbed of his grandfather's truck,
he absorbs explosions over the bay,

his mind alive in a vivid world
of battling boys, colonial wars,
and threats he cannot name.

Oh, where are you now as the wars roll on?
Out past the narrows, out past the spit, out past
the long tongue of wild stars whispering,
Goodnight, little ones, goodnight.

The Renewal of All Things

Remembering red lights and the vacant roar
of mainland life, our five-year-old son
Elias proclaims, "The thing about islands
is you can go where you go. There aren't
many crosswalks."

Feet set free, we've escaped to Chebeague
his sister observing her very first birthday,
her blue eyes bright, her face a smear of frosting.
With toys in hand, Elias is launching
        A Love Sale in Lego City.

Part salesman, part brother, he declares
"I'm part climber," then assumes divine
meteorological powers, announcing
"We've got to try to bring
the weather to its senses."

Evening comes, opening her palms,
as we await the renewal of all things:
a moment alone in the field again
forgetting ourselves, awash in a sea
of gratitude, where all there is
is wind in the pines, whispering crickets,
the plum purple sky at night.

Spirits of the Island Cottage

Fireflies hang lanterns out in the meadow
though they won't come around our cities anymore.
Our porch lights flicker, calling home the caravans
of mendicant moths who find their rest
against the breast of the screened front porch
        facing the mouth of the sea.

Everywhere birdsong welcomes us home:
chickadee chatter, the gossip of sparrows,
hummingbirds hovering, whirring, diving,
thrusting their delicate swordfish beaks
into the sweetwater hanging
        just beyond our window.

Generations before us have called this place home:
the scent of cedar, wood smoke, the shore.
In the fireplace they left a bronze medallion
with Twelve Steps reminding us
        Live and Let Go.

Like branches of family, like rosebush and pine,
the cottage limbs stretch in every direction:
toward a front yard where children build Fenway Park,
toward a beach hiding relics of World War II.

Painted blue stars whirl round the rafters,
singing in time with scratchy old vinyl,
honey pouring from the radio's lips.
Our baby eats pancakes, mostly butter it seems,
        stabbing her feet into her grandmother's shoes.

All's quiet at night, save for the sound
of crickets and a phantom gramophone playing
Ziegfeld & Garland, Gershwin & blues.
Our newspapers flip softly, the ballgame's on low.
       In the dark of the kitchen, a blue pilot light shines.

The House That Elias Built

At the garden's edge, a monarch butterfly and swallowtail
circle the outfield as our daughter Ruthanna takes her first steps,
    rooting hard for the home team.

Her brother Elias hatches his plans as I climb the mound
and the crowd goes wild, the crickets roar,
    mourning doves call for the umpire's head.

Out in the woods the bets are placed, the treaties made,
spies and thieves are laying their traps while sailors are singing
    Take Me Out to the Old Ball Game.

The fallen boulders of ancient walls grin through a veil
of moss and fern. Their time is now, they won't be moved.
    The young and old stand firm.

The crowd grows quiet. The teams return: the Philadelphia
Buster-Rockets versus the Freedom Fighters of Washington.
    As the home team ace named Jason Dirt, I pitch to my son,

Matt the Hat, with Ezekiel Momer—the one they call Homer—
waiting on deck, and Myson Willies warming up in the pen.
    Far from here, the Red Sox play and desert wars rumble

but for one brief moment, the garden's a ballpark,
    the boy its builder, the daddy his servant, the trees all ears.

The temple fires are burning low,
    and soon the summer is whispering
        all the innocence we can bear.

Small Wildlife Observed While Sitting with Ruthanna on an Island Lawn

There's a certain species
of mercy that appears
when our soft gaze
hits the meadow just so
revealing
a caterpillar: holy, complete
eking her way over summer grass
blade upon blade
over mountains, through valleys of stone.

Cave Painting

Wrapped in a blanket of armor from Hudson Bay
my wife rests, observing her Becca-nap beside the fire,
her long arms crossed in fetal-position,
her feet shrouded in wool.

In the room next door, our son leaps high
over the bed like an acrobat in a circus tent
as silver clouds make way for the stars.

Across the hall, our daughter rests, singing in tongues,
flipping the pages of her little book, grasping at words
as seabirds evade the blanket of rain.

The boy creeps in and scales the couch
arms stretched over his mother's head
like a peregrine falcon watching her young.

In the cave of the chimney, fire licks the soggy embers
while far from here in a forest in France
we're told our ancestors played the flute
on a delicate lightning bolt of bone

as the Ice Age thawed and hunters discovered
the lure of music, a membrane stretching
from here to beyond, and then, as now,
        the mother rose slowly to stir the fire.

The Varied Meanings of Green

Lying in the wide green field of his mind,
his baseball mitt nearby, our three-year-old son
rolls over to say: "Something tells me
        the world never changes."
"What is it?" I ask, and he pauses a moment
to ponder the sky. "I don't know," he replies.
        "It's a secret."

And could it be now, these five years later,
—a green island meadow unfurling before us
with baseball bats and a tattered copy
of *The Hobbit* nearby—could it be now
that his secret lies in the color green,
the way it shines in his eyes, and shines in mine,
as the evening sun somersaults into the trees?

Tethered

The Northern Plains Indians a world away
could teach us that a borrowed tipi requires
a slight lean to balance the wind just so
        and keep the poles from walking away.

A tipi anchors our children here,
gazing over the cottage's shingled roof,
awaiting the silver horn of the moon
and the footsteps of the wandering moose
who came to this meadow, mysteriously,
        the day our son was born.

How strange that a home from the Northern Plains
should come to land off the coast of Maine,
hemmed in by pines and raspberry bush,
tethered to earth to harbor us here,
until the chill winds of autumn come.

To the Tipi in the Island Meadow

In your presence I lean further into my life
to mind the circle that has no end.
At night I listen for screech owls poised
above your threshold, frightening predators,
guarding the guard dogs asleep with their masters,
watching over the children who dream.

In quieter times you can feel the wind stirring
the Tibetan prayer flags that hang from your poles,
a flag for each person sheltering here,
each speaking its own intention.

These flags are wind-horses: prayers of compassion
        galloping out on the breath
with the Four Elements and the Five Pure Lights
over glacial valleys and emerald oceans
toward every hidden corner of the mind.

Tipi, by day you are emptiness, inviting us all
to pause and wonder, yet by night
as the ancestors come out to shine
and smile at your improbable presence here,
your wooden-pole fingers pick up a brush
to paint wisps of mountains and rivers without end
among the snow-capped stars.

Tibetan Prayer Flag

Tied carefully by our uncle, a Vietnam vet
        and map librarian with a master's hand,
the flag hangs low from the top of his tipi
        here as if it's always been
on an island in Maine in the midst of a field
where tiger lilies stop and stare.

It's only one flag, one among many
prayers of nations and rumors of war.
How long, scarlet banner, how long until
you unleash your freedom,
        take to the wind,
                fly into the deep
                        imperturbable blue?

The Empire of Sister Monkey

—Somerville, Massachusetts

On my walk this morning to Porter Square Station
the word *Empire* appeared, spray-painted along
the great granite walls of the underpass
and for some strange reason its elegant script
reminded me not of cruelty or stone
in ancient Byzantium or Rome,
but of the soft hidden life
of my son's Sister Monkey, stuffed animal companion
from long ago, hibernating alone through a winter in Maine,
not lost as we'd feared, but at home in the darkness
of the shuttered cottage, breathing the silence,
nestled at the bottom of the bedsheets where
our son's feet sleep in summertime.

Our Son's Ninth Birthday, Observed with Chinese Poetry

Afraid to awaken the people of heaven
as Li Po warned us centuries ago

I perch at the edge of a quiet meadow
as the fireflies prepare to shine.

Through distant trees a lavender layer
of dusk hovers over the emerald sea.

Our son Elias plays *Taps* on his trumpet,
summoning the living to his baseball game.

Shaking off our slumber, we slide on mitts,
lazy bodies greeting the afternoon.

In the kitchen his birthday cake is rising
like an Aztec sun from a golden sea,

smiling as eons of day and night whirl over
the volcanic cliffs of Deer Point.

I pause and bow, remembering now
the crushed blue snake we found in the dirt

and buried under moss and morning glories.
The sky implores benevolence

toward the boy, his sister, each one of us
—so many billions shining now—

joy blossoming from our lips, along our brows,
awakening the fireflies out in the meadow

their song a quiet waterfall
cascading from the plum tree of heaven.

Pondering July as the Light Crawls across the Grass

In the risen season, fireflies climb the length of my arm
wondering what human flesh is. A choir of cicadas
freezes time, and my mind spools back to childhood
when cicada skeletons littered the alley
at the cracked foot of our block.

In the risen season there's no reason or rhyme
for the crazymad love of my daughter who's bouncing
along the zipline from this life to that.
I'm at her command, flying over the creek,
dodging the claws of the hemlock tree.

In the risen season, there's no comprehending
the beauty of birches and lilies that lean
like musical notes in a tangle of brambles and dirt.
Tonight the lilies burn heavy and bright,
looming large in the story of my parents' first love
where wildflowers erased the fissures of fear.

So tonight I'll bathe in a cascade of roses,
the sky as gold as the sabbath candle,
the clouds leaving traces of the holy,
the full moon floating its prayerful balloon
as the ten thousand fireflies shine.

My Daughter Ruthanna's Names for Snails on a Hike to Little Chebeague Island

She calls them
        Buttercup and Samson,
                Max, Rosa, and Bob

hiding beneath their delicate shields
        at the foot of a tree named
                Esmeralda.

They call her
        little one, beloved,
                home.

They call her
child of the world.

Lost on the Little Island

If I told you that low tide exposes a naked spit
and you could walk over the sand to the other island
        would you follow me to Little Chebeague?
If I told you that invasive species would curl their tongues
that chokeberry and poison oak lie in wait
would you walk this path with me?
If I told you that my children and I would leave
their mother sitting in a pool of shade beneath a spruce
and we'd traverse the ruins of a clamshell path
past the cavernous cellar of the burnt hotel
and deserted cottages of the naval base
with empty eyes and phantom floors
        would curiosity or fear draw you in?

If I told you then that my barefoot boy
would cut his foot upon a rock
that he and his sister would cry and cry
as if abandoned to the night
how would you counsel me then?
If I told you fear is another name
for parched summer grass and endless paths
        would you question my resolve?
If I'd known then that their mother would run
in panic along the silent trails
that we'd yell for help until the tide came in
that we'd stagger along the northern shore
past the ghosts of Union veterans
and silent Victorians in summer hats and parasols
past cannons firing for the Fourth of July
        would you follow me there and back?

If I told you my wife began to plan a nautical rescue
and if I said my son's name is Elias the Bold
and my daughter I call Ruthanna of Nine Lives
would it all cohere, would it all make sense?
If I told you we'd reach the vanishing point
before the isthmus disappeared beneath high tide
and we'd see my wife running, waving an orange towel *SOS*,
and our arms would be strengthened
by bearing the weight of our children,
        would you believe me then?

III

Awaiting the Doctor's News

We are oblivious to the beauty surrounding us:
out in the meadow the children at play
tongues of lightning over the water
blue dragonflies spinning their wands.

From the high thin air, tenterhooks dangle:
the telephone's become my enemy,
all power out in the distant city
where the beloved lives.

Is it any wonder that the screech of saws,
the wailing dogs, old rugs hung out in the field to dry
draw my anxious eye to the circle of stones
where the children's campfire burns?

Sadness hobbles down the muddy road
to the curiosity shop in the Island Grange
with the bloodied raincoat
and the discount today:

> *Half off on everything*
> *that's blue.*

Coming to Terms

What are we to make of this:
a smooth-fashioned cabinet,
a ghost story, a song?

What are we but dust from dust
spare flecks of gold
in the creek?

And what are we to do with our loves:
draw canyons or swim, drag comfort
smoldering from the fire?

Who are we but supplicants pleading
please, please
take this cup from my lips

but if you cannot, then help me to bear it
with whatever strong grace
this moment requires.

What then shall we say
what more might we do
as the beloved swims too far from the shore?

Some Things I Know to Be True

I am alive for now

Breath slides into the troubled ocean
        of my buttoned-down Oxford shirt

The pale buttons look like the eyes of a ghost

Illness has come—
        and news travels down the worry-vine

I'm paralyzed in this place of worry,
        praying it turns to awe

This morning the soles of my shoes met the woods,
        the woods replied *Hello*

There is One who is near us,
        who will guide us if we wait

Be still and wait,
        as the early Quakers reminded us

wait and see that you keep to the Guide,
        wait as if lost in the woods at night

eyes adjusting to the dark, knowing
        there's knowledge far deeper than fact

sure as green moss beneath your feet.

Family Health Crisis, Day Three

A quaking aspen high above the meadow here,
        but not so far as the sea.
Clustering leaves at right angles to earth
appear precarious, holding on to life
at the summer peak of their strength.

They're like a climber's fingers scratching granite
at the very point where we must decide
to move or to lie—dead still in midair—
defying all laws of gravity
or to turn the corner and wrestle past
what has kept us from finding center.

And yet we remember the whole is held
by an invisible thread linked to a tree,
deep-rooted in earth, waving in innocence
as if everything
        somehow
              will be
                      alright.

Pearl of Great Price

Out in the meadow a pearl of great price:
        dewdrop glistening on the razor tip
                of one lone blade of grass.

Flashing a signal *SOS*, it's stranded
        on an island in midsummer heat
                with nowhere left to hide.

If I choose to approach, will it disappear?
        Better to wait and watch from a distance,
                listening to its plenitude.

There's a vanishing always
        when you close your eyes
                then open them wide:

fear receding, and all that remains
        is quiet and sunlight
                and one lone blossom of orange.

Anatomy of Yes

Yes:
Three intimate letters like dinner shared
with mama, baby, and me

Yes says the quaking aspen waving
by the island meadow at dusk

Yes, yes
my Muslim brother, my Jewish sister:
two scripts, one common tongue

Yes, honey baby, everything truly
is alright, not *will be* ... not *sometime* ...
but *now!*

Yes, yes
Y yes ... *E* yes,
and yes, especially *S*:

Yahweh, Elohim, Shekinah
burning in the Shabbat candle,
light as rain
speaking light into life
nothing less
        than the infinite

How beautiful the beloved answering
the body of night
with a lullaby: *Yes*

your lips the sole song
on which all things depend.

Soundings from Chebeague

If an island could speak, what might it say
        and if listening, what might we hear?

Restless bare feet
        running on gravel

or the squish of new pavement
                along North Road

The quiet of the Grannell Cottage
                awakening
    white as enamel
        a molar glistening in morning light

The soft contraction
    of wet towels drying:
        a reminder of yesterday's joy

The silence of guns
        in the gravel pit

The word "Where?" stretched out by a lobsterman
        grown to three syllables at least.

The puttering motors of fishing boats
        as lobsters plot their escape

The mourning dove
    and the murder of crows
        demanding new food to eat

The crunch of seagrass
        and the panting dog's tongue

The blue heron's complaint
        when startled from stillness
                and her great one-legged last stand

The chatter of brooks
        sharing yesterday's news
                from deep within the aquifer

The Wabanakis' eternal song
        and the cry of an island
                as sea levels rise

The thunder of ice floes the size of New Jersey
        breaking off from the coast
                of Greenland last week

and the sound of our returning
        to the cottage by the creek:
                the clicking of Legos
                      on the hardwood floor

as our children create a new world.

The Pie Sale Fundraiser

The room opens, full of light, and the gatekeepers
of the Library and Island Hall, suntanned teens,
hand you your tickets for benefit pie
to build their new skating rink. Onstage
a young man is channeling Springsteen,
a sinister tale of Atlantic City, as far from here
        as the moon or the Cape of Good Hope.

From the bustling kitchen the pies unfurl
as primal offerings to the night:
apple, raspberry, chocolate, and rhubarb.
The coffee is hot, the air thick with rain,
        the room smells of old love and new.

Up front the grandmothers are herding children
as old men smile beneath baseball caps.
With their one guitar Amanda and Tiffany
conjure the ghosts of country music:
Appalachia adrift in the Atlantic tonight,
the muse of Patty Loveless summoning
each lonely note, reminding us all
        that life is the most precious thing.

The building shudders with raucous applause
as a boy takes the stage with his father in tow.
Together they sing, calling down the spirit,
down from the prairies of Ontario,
Neil Young's "Old Man" looking at our lives,
        our grays and our gold,
the Island Hall murmuring assent,
        rain cleansing the darkness from our roof.

World in Flight

In the morning, our seven-year-old daughter ascends
to her prickly perch in the arms of the pine,
where I watch her reach for the wooden grips,
and with two quick cries, hers and mine,
she leaps from her fortress into the wind,
pouring her life down the cool steel wire
of her grandfather's zipline over the world,
down past the fruit trees over the fern,
waving farewell to pine needles and rain,
suspending time as if this day, as if this child,
as if this green could last, please God,
       just one long moment more.

Grandparents, Salvaging

Their sacred duty, she explains,
is to patrol the beach for plastic and glass
castoffs of a wanton world, and so they walk—
grandmother Beth crowned in white,
her husband Superman in a fedora—
each with a bag, this island, their home,
which salvaged their lives from the empty nest,
gathering up whatever sharp things
might threaten the blue heron as she descends
        with cries as old as morning light.

Providence Chooses the Great Blue Heron

Last night at sunset an hour before dinner
I watched the heron ready his sword
alone in his dapper evening garb.

Lord of his manor, aglow on the shore
he strode, content, with his monocled eye
far more patient than I.

Awaiting our feast, I knew I'd be fed
—no, stuffed beyond satisfied—
but privation has its way with me

a residue from the ancestors
who clung to spears, hunting prey
along the frozen tundra.

The heron with his elegant, purposeful neck
glances down at his timepiece, watching, waiting,
       trusting the ocean will always provide.

Vacation Choreography, Extended Family

Each one knows our scripted part:
the uncle who steps to the badminton net
the cousin who comforts the younger one
the choreography of a table set,
a feast unleashed with lobster eyes
peering from the bright blue bowl.

Each one writes our character's lines:
the quiet readers who hit home runs,
the puzzlers, the makers of Fourth of July floats,
the tipi builders and tenders of fire,
s'more roasters, lone singers, night owls.

Each one dances or waits in the wings:
the prodigal elder, the jumpers through hoops,
the kayakers, wanderers, wielders of big boats,
star gazers, ballplayers, dish doers, day done –
all now returning to our rest
behind the velvet curtain of night.

Mystery

The July sun is withering
up by Calder's Clam Shack
as if we, like the scallops,
were adrift, and deep in the fryer.

My limbs are scarred an angry red
by surly mosquitoes and the lesions left
by broken shells and barnacles
from yesterday's swim in the sound.

As we walk together down the long green tunnel
of Carter's Point Road, under telephone
wires swaying like a fisherman's net,
I'm thinking again of the strange new world

of the wandering prophet from Galilee—
how I might spend a lifetime
and not comprehend, and then
the familiar whisper comes:
Is the mystery not enough?

Secret Dreams

Above the treeline the silver-bearded Milky Way
        sits with Cassiopeia in her chair,
                the Big Dipper pouring them a cup of night

Like a wounded animal, the ocean is loping
        back to the deep
                and the tick tock tick of the clock on our wall

calls dreams into being, the porch light inviting
        our darkness inside. The children
                sleep under patchwork quilts

of earth and sky and sea.
        Peepers and crickets draw near to listen
                for foxes, deer, and the vagabond moose

while we wait for the wilderness to whisper to us
        in secret dreams,
                parceling night into now, now, and then.

Vertigo-Proof

In the newspaper I spied a strange exhibit:
the darkened worlds of the Wyeth men
in vertiginous angles and bird's eye views,
their oil paint splattered like bruises along
the shattered coast of Maine.

Dizzy is the raptor's bloodshot eye
cast along the museum wall
beside a sinking skiff, a drowning man,
a seagull captured mid-scream.

Yet here on an island many miles away
our daughter flies high, so high up above
the creek on a rope swing—no malice today—
only question upon question, until finally she asks,
"What is marriage like?"

Living History

A rarity: my wife and I alone with our daughter
Ruthanna as our son travels south to D.C.
to witness the March on Washington
50th anniversary. Driving north we discover
a museum of old homes clustered together,
and Ruthanna enters her element,
        her blue eyes gathering light.

Following her lead, we stroll along the victory gardens
from World War II and discover a dime store
with the goods that fed my father's childhood:
penny candies in great glass jars, Quaker Oats,
Nabisco crackers, familiar names to fill rationed lives.
A mannequin cashier wears my grandmother's dress.
        Whose history lives in me?

We travel on to Durham, Maine, a bed & breakfast
farm & inn, built by settler colonists as a place of firsts:
first town meeting and house of worship,
a first escape for Ruthanna, her mama, and me.
        Who then will remember our history?

In the backyard pasture, the great wide eyes
of alpacas smile: dark universes suspended
over frumpy old bodies, theirs and mine,
        all chewing from the same emerald cud.

Unknowing at the Shaker Village, and Other Secrets of Maine

I did not know that by the early twentieth century,
the Shaker community at Sabbathday Lake
was making candy, relying on the sweet teeth of the world
to earn their daily bread. Nor did I know that a smile could turn
as curiously sweet as Sister Frances's, sitting beside her Sister June,
watching a crafts market on the lawn, where neighboring tribes
sold baskets and bracelets, drummed and danced, singing songs
of creation, healing, and hope.

Before I met these living Shakers, I did not know their ancestors
painted furniture brightly and acquired the latest appliances
to draw converts toward a more beautiful life.
I never suspected that inventiveness came
as a gift of freedom in community,
freed to create new seeds, fine chairs,
and efficient hooks in every room.

Until we stayed in a country inn not far from where the Shakers live,
I did not know that Spielberg saw in alpacas' eyes
the wise gaze that became his Extraterrestrial,
and until I sat and watched these creatures
roaming a pasture in the afternoon sun,
spitting out hay and chewing up time,
I knew nothing of alpacas at all.

Child of privilege on the lam, I never imagined I'd wander the aisles
of an outlet store, and suddenly discover I have all I need,
then leave that place empty-handed and free.
Nor did I know the freedom of glaciers, crawling back
to their homes so many thousands of years ago,
leaving knuckles of mountains in their wake,
to form the islands of Maine.

And how could I know that freedom rolled through
the town of Brunswick where locals say the Civil War began
the morning that Harriet Beecher Stowe had a vision
of a bondsman as she sat in her pew in the village church,
and her great novel began to unfold.
The war ended, they say, the day that Joshua Lawrence
Chamberlain, mustachioed hero of Gettysburg,
then governor and president of the college here,
received the surrender at Appomattox
before coming home to this quiet pew
in this church in Maine, a sunlit place
he knew so well.

Rope Swing

With a flick of her chin, she defies all laws of gravity
flying high above a menacing creek
beyond the hemlock and giant beech
with its ragged arrowhead leaves.
Our daughter Ruthanna in a turquoise dress
like my grandmother's, a Valentine's gift,
her eyes fixed wide, her bare feet spanning
a continent: island, mountains, prairie, sea
then back to the forest where evergreens sway
and the evening sun comes out to play,
casting its shadows over the creek
like splotches on a snow leopard's back.

"Your love keeps lifting me higher and higher,"
we harmonize as she soars with each new push:
a call and response, a girl, her dad, and the spirit
whistling through twilight trees,
singing us back through the years between,
laughing over the menacing creek.

Life of the Insects

The mosquitoes are biding their angry time,
buzzing our ears like the electric guitars
of the punk rock gods in Fort Reno park
not far from my childhood home. Their neighbors
the crickets sing our children to sleep.
Will they ever remember our names?

Inside our tents, the earwigs wait with sharpened claws
while sand fleas snap their wicked fingers as if to say:
Alright, you humans, show us some succulent flesh.
Up at the Clam Shack, shoo-flies are circling the dirty lips
of garbage bins, licking mustard and whatever remains of the day.

Horseflies divebomb as they did in the swimming hole
at my grandparents' orchard, waging war as we swam
through lilies and algae, beneath the rotting diving board.
When twilight came, the fireflies hung their Japanese lanterns
to float among the cherry trees.

At bedtime now we leave the porch lights on
for the monarch butterflies and luna moths
to dry the dewfall from their wings,
and welcome the ancestors who visit our dreams.

What do these insects see in the dark, as bats swoop overhead?
Are we islands of heat or lantern light,
or are we simply the slightest wind
        brushing their wings as we pass?

Luna Moths Visit the Island Cottage

Each morning another one appeared
until they nearly had us trapped,
afraid to open the screen doors where
they spread their dusty wings to dry,
afraid to disturb their rest.

In darkness they would rise from dirt beneath
our window sills to assume their place
beside the monarch butterflies
drawing night into their wings.

It was moonlight that called them,
pooling over the meadow, the harbor, the sea,
and the moon draws us too,
each a visitor passing through,
waiting for darkness to open our wings.

Old Dog Days

In the distance the chainsaws
register their bitter complaints
as bulldozers bore holes
in the great gut of the forest.

In our kitchen, a chorus
of old dogs is singing
like salty mariners wandering
through a sea of human legs.

Black Lucy's shoulder is shorn of hair,
her abscess a mountain of needlepoint.
Ollie the golden retriever limps,
quiet on arthritic hind legs.

Seeking Peter, his master, Ollie finds
affection from a nearby rocking chair.
Mac, a splash of black and white,
greybeard gossiping with the birds,

sidles up to Doc, his owner and friend,
arranging a row of medicine
like a nurse in an old folks home.
How much like us these old dogs are:

resplendent with our silver beards,
new hips, love handles, our bright faces shorn
of cancerous cells from the heat of summers past.
The love comes simple now: meat on a plate,
        fresh water from a silver dish.

Supper with You

—Central Provisions Restaurant, Portland, Maine

Years inched forward, our children grew,
and we found our places leaning in toward evening
under timber beams and a silver ceiling of corrugated tin.
Your face was a smile, your eyes a blue harbor
and the walls spoke quietly of families and strangers,
tenderness on every plate. As you rose to wash
your hands, my mind grew still in wonder
        at the gasp of sunlight
glancing through the frosted glass,
casting strange colors around the room.
Traces of radiance spilled over your seat
and I heard the word, the whisper within,
saying *You are being loved* and I knew
        we'd come to this place before.

Dignity of Work

Highfalutin', that's what I was, as I scrubbed the table
after supper in Maine, and spoke of the dignity of work.
My wife laughed out loud at the utter pretense
of wrapping myself in the mantle of labor
as if setting the table were equivalent somehow
to picking grapes in the fields of Salinas
or working the looms in the mills of Lowell
or clearing the hardwood forests for roads
in the conscientious objector camps
of the Second World War.

But "falute away" I say and smile, remembering
the Wild Things gnashing their terrible teeth
at Max who refused to do his chores,
remembering too the small satisfaction
of dirt undone, of stains removed or wished away.

Here in the cottage we gather for rest,
between scrubbing the pots and fixing the meals,
and building from nothing Fourth of July floats,
we summer people from somewhere else
laying down for a moment the tools of our trades:
carpenters, dressmakers, writers, and builders,
crunchers of numbers and daycare providers,
fixers and helpers of every sort, remembering once more
the great work that sabbath rest is.

What Lives in the Winter Wall

The summer our daughter performed *Little Mermaid*
we were proud, so proud she stepped into the breach
to play Prince Eric when the lead fell sick.

In her black sash and ponytail, Ruthanna sang out
as every kid-creature of the deep drew near
and her parents came up for air.

Not long after, on an island in Maine, we drove past
a wall of lobster traps, yellow & green,
on the twisting road to Deer Point.

Each winter these cages lie in wait among the pines,
before returning to the deeps to lure fresh victims
into their kitchens to enjoy the fish-carcass bait.

But tonight I wonder, will we who remain
among the living, above the sea, will we
claim our freedom when summer comes?

Will we assume new crowns and write new scripts,
burst free from every cage and snare,
beyond the winter walls?

Their Quiet Bedrooms

are not so different from the ones we knew
in Appalachia where our grandparents lived
in a little brick farmhouse above the world.

As children we'd watch the ivy climb
the forest walls, creeping its fingers down corridors,
while here on the island our children sleep
as lavender roses bloom in the dark.

Summer rains danced on our silver roof then,
the scent of apples filling our room, but tonight
bats skitter over the meadow, and heat lightning
conjures pirate ships up from the deeps.

At our grandparents' home, our bodies would ache
after days of work in the orchard packhouse,
scratching at peach fuzz and the early
adolescence under our skin.

When my eyes shut tight in that brick bedroom,
the great white tongue of the conveyor belt
would spit rivers of peach, peach upon peach,
far more than our feverish hands could sort.

Down in the valley, bloodhounds would wail,
and the hunters' gunfire punctured our dreams
but tonight on the island, the lobster boats putter
in with their haul. The wolf moon waves good night.

Afraid of the darkness, I would elbow my brothers,
as news of the death squads in El Salvador
murmured up from the TV in the parlor below.

Here on the island our son is practicing algebra,
our daughter exploring new worlds of myth
as British broadcasting brings wars to their ears.
        Screen porches are always porous.

Quaking Aspen

What is it about you, quaking aspen,
that calls to me: your permanence and fixity,
your visual jazz and levity, tapping the winds
like cymbals or piano keys, or is it the way
your leaves move like hummingbirds' wings,
so fast they're hardly there?

Perhaps your call comes from the land of dreams,
recalling the nights I spent in Haiti that year
among earthquake survivors sleeping in tents,
afraid the roofs would collapse.

Our hosts ushered us into revival each night,
the holy ghost thundering through drums and bass,
a preacher's voice roaring, a great power pouring
along the aisles and for a moment, we were not afraid.

Together we moved in a rhythm of freedom
and the aftershocks were no obstacle now
as we danced and the winds in the quivering palms
swept tears from every eye.

In Maine tonight, the meadow fills with fireflies
as night strolls in past the sculpted cedars,
their leaves like spear tips defending our gates,
and I wonder what leads one aspen to wave
and another to rest, quiet and waiting,
and a third to shout glory among the ruins?

IV

Jazz Trio at the Island Church

One Sunday morning an island awoke
to a drummer on fire with rim shots, brushstrokes,
and a hi-hat ringing, a pianist's nimble fingers singing
as the old folks stood and danced down the aisles
and the jubilant mother and captain's son
lit the altar candles while the people sang, oh how they sang,
as their ancestors had in the days when preachers
plied the green waters off the coast of Maine,
singing "Amazing Grace" and "Shall We Gather
at the River" the beautiful the beautiful river they sang
as if the scales had fallen from their eyes
with every tear washed out to sea and they prayed
how they prayed, there was no need to preach,
joy was all there was to say, and when the time came
for the benediction, an elder rose beside the altar
gazed over his glasses and out to the sea
raised his hands and prayed from the prophets Isaiah,
Ezekiel, and John Coltrane and the islanders danced
oh how they danced, like my grandmother Miriam
beside the Red Sea, dark water crashing
on the far shore beyond them, proclaiming *Yes
there will be* singing over Jordan when we arise,
with the Spirit blossoming the August air,
singing Amen Amen Amen Amen
to all you who refuse to fear.

The Soul Put Back Together

There's a flurry of music over the water
        and the black-eyed Susans lean in to listen,
                bending their golden ears.

Down by the inn
        an island band is singing slow
                the Beatles' plea to "Come Together"

as the bride and groom
        begin their dance.
                The world is a river of dreams.

Here in the cottage
        our daughter sleeps,
                dreaming of islands and castles of sand.

I recall the words she shared before bed:
        "We're going to the west of the day,
                surviving."

Dusk comes aching through the pines,
        the tipi is empty out in the meadow,
                bats swoop overhead.

A silver moon crawls across my beard,
        an old truck shudders
                down Carter's Point Road.

How long since I've been
        down the Shenandoah Valley?
                How far to my grandfather's mountain?

The Peacemakers

On the bright clapboard wall facing North Road
a gold-lettered sign reads *Chebeague United
Methodist Church, Built in 1855.*
Fishermen, farmers, homemakers, and captains
fashioned this place in the decade before
the island men went south to war.
Indoors the darkness smells of life—fertile, musty
like an old pine cabinet or chest of drawers—
a cool cavern with lanterns humming
above the names of those who gave
so the island might do the work of healing,
binding up the wounds, burying the dead.

Today we proclaim good news to captives,
release for the poor, the mystery of the risen life.
Forgiveness is the needful word, aglow in that old
familiar painting of the dreamy Jesus from the 1940s
that shines as it did in my grandparents' church
on Willow Hill in the Blue Ridge Mountains
and ten thousand other hamlets of worry and need.

What the Mountains Say

At Calder's Clam Shack on the island of Chebeague
the lawn is a great green palm stretched out
and its tents are places of sacrifice.

When evening comes, fireflies keep the candles burning,
and my daughter walks toward the setting sun,
then beyond to the beach where the islanders say

on a clear day you can see all the way to New Hampshire
and Mount Washington's steadying peak.

So now I wonder as night rolls in, when morning comes
and silver dew splashes the sleep from my eyes,
if I squint might I glimpse the Blue Ridge mountains

I knew as a child, and might I remember
the strange and distant beauty that is
trying once more to save my life?

Captain Watches the Stars

Alone on an island dock and watching
the silver syrup of galaxies
I imagine the mariners long ago
peering through their astrolabes
to navigate life by mystery.

What patient, quiet, contemplative gaze
the night required to make their way
to the far country alive?

But tonight our century is thick with the presence
of silhouettes crowned by meteors,
squinting toward distant light.

A ferry captain ambles towards us pointing
Look there! and as we follow his finger,
counting to ten, the night breaks open
with a sudden flash and the Space Station thrusts
its silver mass across the blue firmament of heaven.

At 17,000 miles an hour, it orbits Earth every
92 minutes, harvesting lettuce to feed us all
five hundred years from tonight.

Disappearing in the shadows of the moon,
all's quiet again, and as we turn toward home,
we spy the Great Bear and Orion the Hunter
lumbering through the wilderness above.

Whiteness Afloat on Summer Vacation

I can't breathe when I think how we came to this place
and to a rock you cannot destroy.
In our canoes, we watch the tide roll out,
thick fingers of seaweed snarling our way
while overhead the white gulls scream
over carcasses of mussels and crabs.
When we reach the tip of Division Point,
I rest my head on a life preserver, but a chill
surrounds me, and my blond and blue-eyed son
Elias is shoving his sister's head into the brine
and we three laugh, spitting up surf,
then suddenly my mind is spiraling back
to my teenage years in Washington, D.C.,
selling dime bags made of oregano
to support our visits to Malcolm X Park
—an open air drug market, now gentrified—
frightened yet trusting we'd somehow be safe
since skin was our get-out-of-jail-free card,
white skin and our cars and letterman jackets,
trench coats and designer acid-washed jeans.
We would graduate prep school and then pass time
at colleges hidden behind ivy brick walls
since whiteness remained our prophylactic,
our coin of the realm saying, Make way world,
we're here, hell bent on rising high
while my Black coworker Anthony Watkins
and our crew of friends we called The Unknowns
would drive home each night to Southeast D.C.
down the long gray tunnel of Connecticut Ave.

angry as hell in a beat-up Dodge, counting the minutes
until sirens would spin and now thirty years later,
I'm floating, he's dead, somewhere out west,
and a sleek black cormorant stands on the pier
with wings wide open to shake off the sea,
as if to say, *Don't shoot.*

Continental Divide

This morning, my chair sat up and spoke:
How long has it been since you visited?

Across the room, a window breathes,
its mouth an astonished "O."

There, beyond us: green daylight, a leaf,
a telephone pole, dark wires joining everything.

There's a Victorian home outside our window
and its square, spare delicacy

it mirrors a house on the island we left,
an ocean of sunlight pouring in

drawing our neighbors nearer to us
through waves of tulips and Japanese maple

but behind our radiator's silver bars,
there's an emerald spot no paint can touch

and on a shelf a toy globe begins to spin,
the green skull of Africa beckoning,

Come, come now, come now and see
the place all life began.

The Ferry to Other Islands

All day long the pull of life, first rising from dreaming
fraught with danger, then a river of berries in my cereal bowl,
then the faces of family: each one no less than miraculous.

Outdoors we hear the cicadas' song, the silence of the hummingbirds,
the crows for once somewhere else. Aboard the ferry, we forget
the stillness of the meadow, and see familiar places anew:

Deer Point's volcanic mysteries, Hope Island a playground
with engine-red barns and forty-some species of tropical birds.
Beyond Hope lies Cliff, an island as village: clapboard houses

leaning into the sun, a library on stilts, a small summer church,
dirt roads, not a car to be seen. As sun sets, we return to Chebeague,
where the islanders wave: two fingers or a palm rising to greet us

from the wheels of jalopies or bike handlebars, passing each other,
stranger, familiar: each one of us careening forward in time
on an island that knows our names.

Deliver Us to Long Island, Maine

Near Katherine's Garden at Harbor de Grace
two bone-white Adirondack chairs sit empty,
perched on a hill of boulders beside
the long apostrophes of silver beech
and I'm wondering whether in these two seats,
enemies might come to sit for a time,
to attend to the inner whisper that says,
Come now friend, let us reason together,
that all might one day be well.

We had ferried over to visit this island
with its crumbling barracks from World War II
and its brownfield sprouting wildflowers
and for some strange reason, my mind rolled back
to the western edge of the continent, where long ago
a Makah Indian village vanished beneath a mudslide
until storm and tide tore the layers away, and I wonder
will we, like the Makah, reach higher ground,
before the gale winds come?

Cobwebs cradle the dew of morning,
as our daughter Ruthanna wades into the surf,
gathering each shard of broken glass.
"We all have to work to make this world
a better place," she declares, beginning here
at Harbor de Grace.

Emergency Mission

First we see them: luna moths in their delicate green
embroidered robes, stranded in branches along the shore,
menaced by seagulls and the rising tide
and the low mutter of ducks in their brooding.

With gentle fingers, my daughter lifts the lime-green moths,
placing them softly among the leaves, as we spy a sailboat
slithering by, its teeth triangular and bright.

Our dog's footsteps fill with the sea, murmuring
as Ruthanna takes charge of the tide
focusing only on her mission of mercy:
saving everything smaller than she is.

Saltwater and sea grass scratch at our shins,
so I hoist her up and we tiptoe together
through the tangled weave of driftwood and roots
to the garden beyond Division Point
where tin pans hang, their sudden bolts
of blinding light driving all predators away.

Island Rescue

—for Andy Grannell

As an island elder, a man from Maine,
he was loath to admit impermanence
despite a doctoral degree in theology,
that is, until one summer day
his breath came sharp, in sudden gusts,
then dropping his tools in the room upstairs
he called out to his brother-in-law for help.
It was sheer providence, he told me later,
a miraculous thing: how the ferry was waiting,
the medics there before you could breathe,
stretcher at the ready to bear him away
across the water, summer tides purring,
the mainland waiting, the arms of a hospital
opening wide, the emergency room doctor
a big Irishman, full of blarney, he said,
explaining the intricacies of the heart.
And then I knew, as never before:
day by day, we are perishing,
day by day, we're being saved.

WHAT THE BODY DOES

Headstones scatter like clamshells across
the yellowing grass of the cemetery yard
while inside the bleach-bone clapboard walls
the ceiling fans swat at the summer air
like slender hands shooing mosquitoes away.

The islanders arrive, undisturbed by time,
find favorite seats and greet their neighbors
with a warm word, a nod, or a smile.
These walls were raised by their ancestors,
whose hymns were much the same.

The choir processes in azure robes
making way for the children of light:
a brother and sister with bright copper hair
lifting their tapers, touching the candles,
pushing the shadows away.

The choir rises to testify that all are welcome here.
In the prayers of the people, the names float up
with gentle commentary from the pews:
sickness, losses, tall tales, and laughter.
Good news comes easy, as if in the uttering of each name
the blind have sight, the wounded will walk,
the kin-dom of healing draws near.

Island Archaeology

One day on the shore my spouse Rebecca
discovered a tiny clay pipe in a hidden place
then her mother Beth found a bottle of wine
with a mysterious message from young German
travelers greeting the world on their journey home,
not far from the beach where rusted sea nets
crawl over the sands like spiders' legs,
where once they kept German U-boats at bay.

Nearby we discover giant white roots
like dinosaur bones, while Addie our niece
keeps her eyes peeled like clementines,
and leaps into the waves, trolling for pirate loot.
Will she find instead, after a storm, the clamshell
middens of the Wabanaki tribes, or campfire circles
with tools and burnt animal bones?

When I was a child I longed to see more
than anything the evidence of how things were,
layers reaching beyond the earth's core, escaping
in ancient civilizations the loneliness of my present.
At midlife now, I sift the sands and wonder whether
anyone can tell us how long the broken sea glass floats
before it reaches the shore?

Self inside Self

There's a loneliness you feel from the outside in
when you're accustomed to being a larger voice
yet here among family you sit back and watch,
listening to the elders sharing their stories,
their laughter and instructions.

From the vantage of your summer chair
beneath the white pine, you hear Addie & Isaac
racing wildly around the yard. "Get me a chair,"
Addie demands, but Isaac replies, with sword in hand,
"I'm not your serf. I'm not your fetchy boy."

Oh self inside self, be free, free
free as the tips of their fighting sticks,
free beyond the loudest voice, to be who you are:
contemplative filled with gratitude
nonviolent footsoldier of social change
round-bellied man just awakening now
to the gracious middle of your life.

Nighttime before the Sea Levels Rise

If you lean in to look
      the ocean at night is indigo
           filled with ten thousand phosphorous stars.

Phosphorous stars and a silent moon
      illumine the shore from which we watch
         two tall ships sailing home.

Two sailing ships oblivious
      to watchers on the shore.
           Three island huts swaying on stilts,

a mirror image of quivering trees
     and heron's feet,
         their melody quiet blue.

Quiet are the eyes
      peering through night: a bat, an owl,
           three islands swept in lunar light.

In lunar light, the islands rise
      like pyramids or humpback whales,
         darkness their silhouette.

Their silhouette, their secrets kept,
      their silent eyes are watching us
         to see what we will do.

The Climate of Maine

"What are you doing?!" my soul demanded
 as blueberries scattered across the floor
 like little landmines, and I was actually
 wondering that myself and wanted to say,
"I don't know, do you?" but instead I said,
"Chill, it was an accident!" and took up
 my broom and gathered those little blue
 planets trapped in jungles of dog hair,
 emptied the maw of my rusty dustpan,
 slunk out the back door, silent, ashamed,
 tiptoeing my way over the parched lawn
 past the clawing hot gusts of August in Maine
 down to the shore, high tide rolling in,
 earth's temperature rising, the wild turkeys blowing
 their angry horns and all I'm asking is,
What are you doing? What the hell,
what the hell are we doing?

"Abide with Us, For It Is the Evening": American Haiku

lavender light before sunrise
yours, mine: a quiet mind
hummingbird awake and watching

                              lingering, one foot out the door
                              eyes wide open, you bathe beneath
                              a purple waterfall of azalea

running for the ferry, late once more,
steps arrested by the orange daylilies
bowing as you pass

                              August haze standing still
                              wingcrash dusk, a broken sky
                              cry of the great blue heron

dewdrop forming on linden leaves,
the sunset a paper lantern swinging
just beyond our reach

Departure

late August ferry
plying gray water
raindrops blurring
the windowpane.
my body wants nothing
of leaving this place.
the bright green buoys
nod *Go* as we pass
bearing all the light
we leave behind.

Beneath the Waves

Kiss me with the kiss of your mouth, the singer of the Song
of Solomon wrote, as if by a kiss, union were mine, as if
in the hummingbird mind at play, in the twilight garden
of earthly delights, there's a quiet place only lovers know.
But oh what happens when the beloved flees
the narrow shell of our life together,
retreating to the far harbor of grief?

We're alone on the ocean blue of the couch,
the sunlight streaming its long yellow tongue,
breathing viral air, but oh, how the window
beckons us both: Escape now, while there's still light,
be gone from these hunkered, darkened rooms
where fear roams at will. And oh how we long
for the eternal Beloved who loves to love,
whose only language is the breath,
promising summer will come again,
a time of singing on the island shore
with the osprey, the eagle, the peregrine falcon,
and the periwinkles waving their tentacles
as if to say, Come away, come away,
beneath the worried waves.

Drop Me in the Water

I asked myself what my prayers look like
and the answer unfolded: it depends on the day,
or the moment really. Sometimes they are
emerald luna moths at night—delicate, dusty—
resting on the threshold of the island cottage,
seeking shelter, or maybe a home—
seeking time enough to dry dew from their wings,
gathering energy to fly when the morning comes.

Sometimes my prayers are another language,
groans and sighs, a keening that looks something
like a lost cat hiding under the porch,
waiting for the rescuer to come.

Sometimes they're like candles in a dark window,
or the raspberry bubbles an infant makes.
Sometimes my prayers assume the shape
of the horn section blowing Al Green's song
"Take me to the river" as I shower
and all the grime of the world
washes away for a moment
and this one grand body—aging, fragile—
burdened with big fat tears for the world—
begins to bounce and dance a bit,
because what more could I do?

Morning Prayer, Chebeague Island, Maine

At the edge of the meadow another chair
       beneath the cedar tree.
A body that might be mine is sitting
in whatever stillness the day allows.
Its sure breath yields a measure of peace
from the battle lines of my mind.

You've said you'll be here in the trench
wherever two or three pitched tent,
but now I am one. Be still, be still
as the supplicants who come into my mind
each with a begging bowl.

From our uncle's tipi, the prayer flags hang
each posing a question:
Why not teach the shadows to dance?
Why not simply sit and watch
the island roses begin to bloom?

Listen to Your Life

The baby's cry and the screech owl at night,
        footsteps along the cabin floor

Listen to your world: dewdrop whispering
        out in the meadow, where everything falls into place

Listen to your dreams: considered, discarded,
        furrows in the garden at the onset of spring

Listen to the wings of the hummingbird seeking
        sweetwater and a soft place to land

Listen to the toy ship in the raspberry patch
        and planes from the arctic high up above

Listen to the world listening to you:
        laughter sailing through the kitchen door,
            songs of children on the road to the sea.

The Shape of Gratitude

Island, it's you who called me
into being. You called me to act,
you made me a home.

A place apart but not so far
we could not see
to the end of the dream.

You, island, you knew our names
before we did: in the murmur of the ferry
and the waves slap-slapping against the pier

as if on drums, and in the squeal of gulls,
and the putter of the lobster boats—
you knew the seagulls' caterwauling

the cricket's whisper behind the leaves
the honey ushering nightfall down
and the morning beckoning, Come,
come see what love will do.

The Island's Reminder

After all the rancor is done,
after the bitter bile of regret has receded
from the narrow cavern of your chest,
after the mosquito storm of worry upon worry
and a thousand things to do, after the fierce
sand pincers of myriad claims
have retreated from the flooded
castles of your mind, go down
to where the water laps
against the shore and bids you *swim*.
Bow down as you pass the blue
delphinium, stacked to the sky
like the Buddhist temples of Kyoto
speckled on the edge of the raspberry patch.

Let one image linger: children chasing fireflies
beside the forest, leaning toward the light.
Let the cool sand dance beneath your toes
and the wind of relinquishment wash all things clean.
Let the generous welcome at the heart of it all
remind you simply whose you are
and how you came to this place.

Notes

What Binds Us to This World (p. 27)
The title comes from a book of poems by Robert Cording.

Chebeague Is an Abenaki Word (p. 28)
In an article titled, "Chebeague Island and the Tides of Time," available on the website of the Island Institute [www.islandinstitute.org], Dana Wilde writes: "The Eastern Abenaki word transliterated 'Chebeague' (pronounced Sha-big) means, according to various sources, either 'wide expanse of water' or 'island of many springs' or 'separated place.'" Other sources suggest "almost separated" as a translation, referencing the way Little Chebeague is accessible by foot from Great Chebeague only at low tide. Some say the name "Chebeague" evolved from *Chebiscodego*, the name used by members of the Wabanaki Confederacy. Other sources state that Chebeague comes from the Abenaki words *T'Cabie* or *Chebidisco*, meaning cold spring, or *Jabeque* or *Gaboag*, meaning separated.

Mysterious Visit of the Moose (p. 31)
Stories of the hero Gluskabe and the moose may be found at [www.native-languages.org/legends]; in *The Faithful Hunter: Abenaki Stories* told by Joseph Bruchac (Greenfield Review Press); and in Bill Haviland's article "Local Indians and the End of the Last Ice Age: Part 1" at [www.abbemuseum.org].

Found Art (p. 34)
The toy ship is an outdoor sculpture by Maine artist Wally Warren.

Island Sabbath (p. 42)
The poem alludes to the healing miracle in Matthew 12:9–13, Mark 3:1–6, and Luke 6:6–11; and also to Matthew 26:11 and John 21:1–14.

THE ETYMOLOGY OF "ACTUALLY" (p. 49)
The inimitable Swedish Chef is a character from Jim Henson's *The Muppet Show*.

LIBERATION OF THE BEACHED WHALE, MULLING VOCATION (p. 59)
In the summer of 1657, a vessel called the *Woodhouse* carried a group of Quaker preachers to Puritan Massachusetts, facing pirates, storms, and persecution. Previously, six of these Friends had been imprisoned by Puritans, banished, and shipped back to England.

OF RACCOONS, MOONS, AND OTHER CREATURES OF THE NIGHT (p. 60)
"Fly Me to the Moon" is a 1954 Bart Howard song popularized by Frank Sinatra. Stanza three alludes to Psalm 74:16, quoted in Dietrich Bonhoeffer's *Life Together*, and also to an ancient Eastern Orthodox way of prayer and to Quaker John Woolman's insight that love is the first motion in pursuing a spiritual leading toward specific action.

MISSING THE CHILD WHO CRIES FOR JUSTICE (p. 62)
Julian of Norwich was a fourteenth-century English mystic and anchoress.

OUR SON'S NINTH BIRTHDAY, OBSERVED WITH CHINESE POETRY (p. 76)
The first line alludes to Li Po's "Written on a Wall at Summit-Top Temple" in David Hinton's translation of *The Selected Poems of Li Po*.

PONDERING JULY AS THE LIGHT CRAWLS ACROSS THE GRASS (p. 72)
The phrase "In the risen season" is from Wendell Berry's poem "Another Sunday Morning Comes," and "traces of the holy" is from the philosopher Emmanuel Levinas.

SOME THINGS I KNOW TO BE TRUE (p. 81)
This poem paraphrases seventeenth-century Quaker Isaac Penington's letter "To Women Friends at Armscot."

PEARL OF GREAT PRICE (p. 83)
The title is drawn from Matthew 13:45–46.

ANATOMY OF YES (p. 84)
In biblical Hebrew, YHWH (Yahweh) signifies the Holy "I Am," Elohim signifies "God," and "Shekinah" signifies "the dwelling or settling of the divine presence."

VERTIGO-PROOF (p. 95)
The painters mentioned are N. C. Wyeth, Andrew Wyeth, and Jamie Wyeth.

LIVING HISTORY (p. 96)
The museum in this poem is Strawbery Banke in Portsmouth, New Hampshire.

UNKNOWING AT THE SHAKER VILLAGE, AND OTHER SECRETS OF MAINE (p. 97)
For more on Wabanaki drumming see [www.themainemonitor.org] and [burnurwurbskeksingers.com].

ROPE SWING (p. 105)
"Your Love Keeps Lifting Me Higher and Higher" was written by Gary Jackson, Raynard Miner, and Carl Smith, and recorded by Jackie Wilson in 1967.

DIGNITY OF WORK (p. 110)
The poem references Maurice Sendak's book *Where the Wild Things Are*.

WHAT THE MOUNTAINS SAY (p. 122)
The final line alludes to Prince Myshkin's assertion that "beauty will save the world" in Dostoyevsky's *The Idiot*, quoted often by Dorothy Day, co-founder of the Catholic Worker movement.

ISLAND ARCHAEOLOGY (p. 132)
This poem draws on an article by Donna Miller Damon for the *Forecaster*, "Maine Bicentennial: Chebeague Island, Part I: Before the Europeans."

"ABIDE WITH US, FOR IT IS THE EVENING": AMERICAN HAIKU (p. 136)
The title alludes to Luke 24:29.

THE SHAPE OF GRATITUDE (p. 142)
The final line paraphrases words from early Quaker leader William Penn.

About the Author

Alexander Levering Kern is a poet, editor, Quaker educator, university chaplain, and interfaith organizer. His work appears in publications such as *Spiritus, About Place Journal, Georgetown Review, Soul-Lit, Spare Change News, The Journal of the American Medical Association* (JAMA), *Consequence Online*, and in anthologies from *Tiferet, Meridian*, Pudding House, and *Ibbetson Street*. He is founding editor of *Pensive: A Global Journal of Spirituality & the Arts* [www.pensivejournal.com] based at Northeastern University, where he also serves as Executive Director of the Center for Spirituality, Dialogue, and Service. Editor of the anthology *Becoming Fire: Spiritual Writing from Rising Generations*, Kern has served and learned alongside communities around the world, including post-earthquake Haiti; post-apartheid South Africa; northern Nigeria; the Middle East; rural Honduras; Hiroshima; Brazil; Ferguson, Missouri; and the Arizona-Mexico borderlands. His family makes their home in Somerville, Massachusetts, and Chebeague Island, Maine, homelands of the Massachusett, Pawtucket, Wampanoag, Nipmuc, and Wabanaki peoples.

Shanti Arts

Nature ▪ Art ▪ Spirit

Please visit us online
to browse our entire book catalog,
including poetry collections and fiction,
books on travel, nature, healing, art,
photography, and more.

Also take a look at our highly regarded art
and literary journal, *Still Point Arts Quarterly*,
which may be downloaded for free.

www.shantiarts.com